JULIUS CAESAR

THE ROMAN GENERAL AND DICTATOR WHO WAS LOVED BY HIS PEOPLE

Biography of Famous People

Children's Biography Books

BABY PROFESSOR

EDUCATION KIDS

Speedy Publishing LLC

40 E. Main St. #1156

Newark, DE 19711

www.speedypublishing.com

Copyright 2017

Julius Caesar was a Roman general and dictator who was best known for bringing the Roman Republic to an end. He was born in Rome, Italy on July 13th, 100 BC and passed away in Rome on March 15th, 44 BC. In this book, you will be learning about his early life and his many achievements.

THE EARLY YEARS

Caesar was born in 100 BC at Subura, Rome as Gaius Julius Caesar. Born to an aristocratic family, his bloodlines were traced to the founding of Rome. While his family was well-off, they were not rich according to Roman standards.

GAIUS JULIUS CAESAR.

He was kidnapped once by pirates when he was still a young man. He joked around with them that he would be able to have them executed when he was set free. They laughed at him, but he then had the last laugh when he captured them later and had them put to death.

DID HE ATTEND SCHOOL?

Gaius started his education when he was about six years old. He was instructed with a private tutor, Marcus Antonius Gnipho and learned to read and write, as well as learning about Roman law and speaking in public. He would need this important skill later in life as the leader of Rome.

BECOMING AN ADULT

When he was sixteen, Caesar's father passed away. He then became head of his family, being responsible for Aurelia, his mother, as well as Julia, his sister. When he was seventeen he married Cornelia, who was the daughter of a powerful Roman politician.

CAESAR'S EARLY CAREER

As a young man, he found himself in the midst of a struggle for power between two government factions. Sulla, the dictator of Rome, whose enemies included both Caesar's father in-law Cinna and Caesar's uncle Marius. He then joined the army and left Rome so that he could avoid Sulla and his followers.

SULLA

CRASSUS

He decided to return to Rome when Sulla died. At that time he was considered a military hero because of his army years. He soon rose up in the ranks of the Roman government and became allies with many powerful men including the Great and wealthy Crassus and the general Pompey. He had become an excellent speaker and the people admired him.

CONSUL AND GENERAL

J ulius was elected as consul when he was 40 years old. This was the highest position of the Roman Republic. This position was similar to a president, however there were two consuls, only serving for a one-year term. When his year as consul came to an end, he became the governor of Gaul.

JULIUS CAESAR ELECTED AS CONSUL

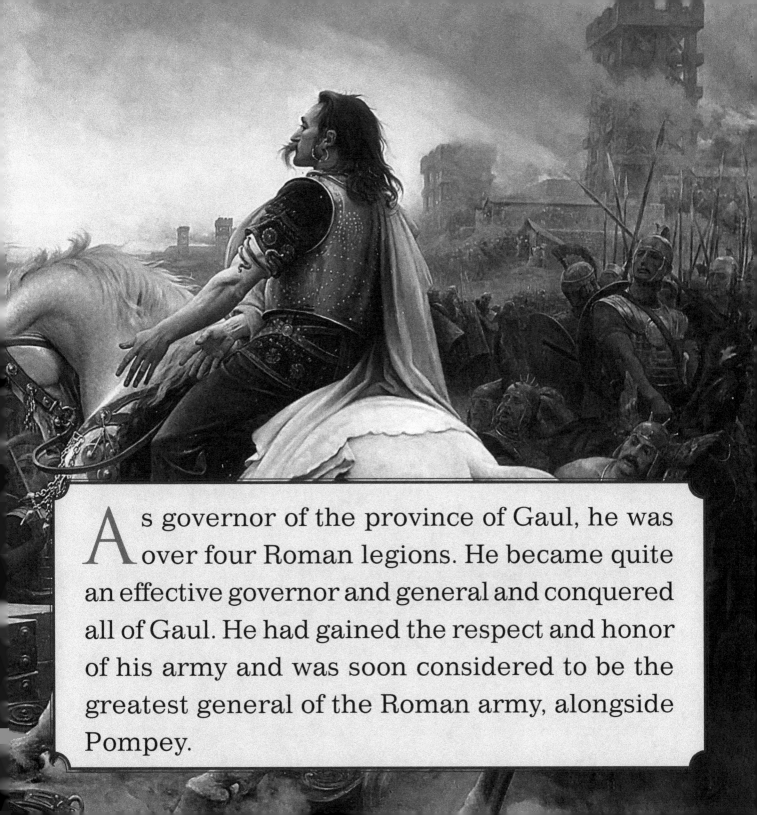

As governor of the province of Gaul, he was over four Roman legions. He became quite an effective governor and general and conquered all of Gaul. He had gained the respect and honor of his army and was soon considered to be the greatest general of the Roman army, alongside Pompey.

CIVIL WAR

The Roman politics became more and more hostile while he was in Gaul. Several of the leaders had become jealous of him and his followers. Pompey even started to become jealous and they soon became rivals. While Caesar had the support of the people, Pompey had support from the aristocrats.

BUST OF POMPEY

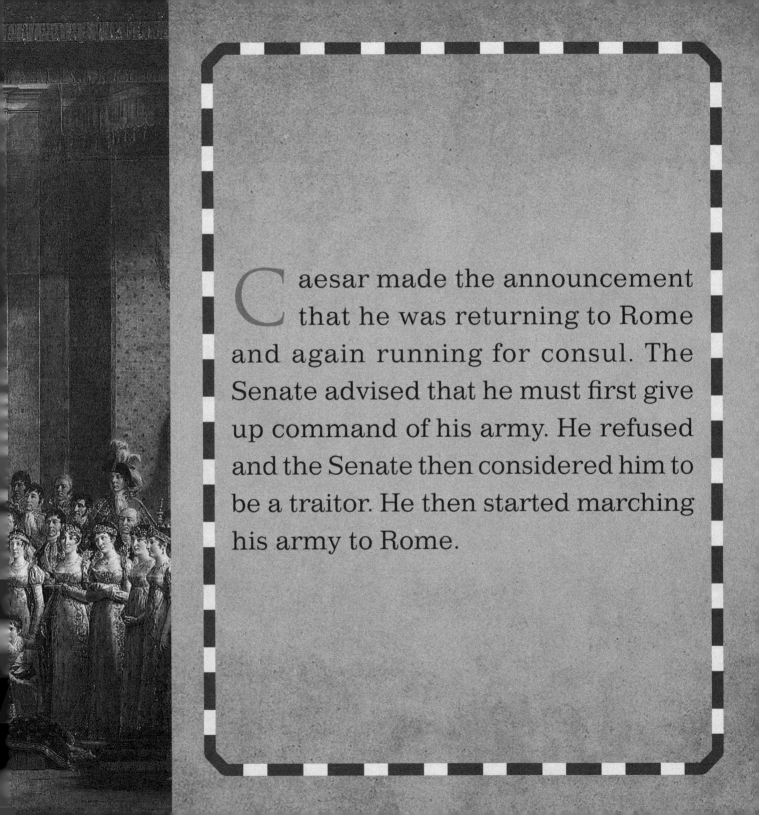

Caesar made the announcement that he was returning to Rome and again running for consul. The Senate advised that he must first give up command of his army. He refused and the Senate then considered him to be a traitor. He then started marching his army to Rome.

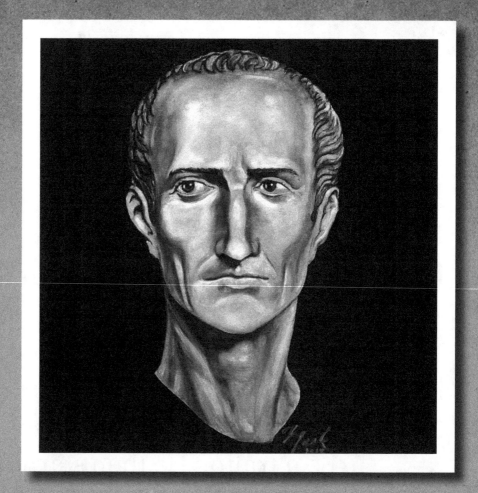

JUIUS CAESAR

In 49 BC, he gained control over Rome, and spent the following 18 months fighting against Pompey. He finally was able to defeat Pompey after chasing him to Egypt.

PTOLEMY VIII

Once Caesar reached Egypt, a young Pharaoh by the name of Ptolemy VIII had Pompey killed and presented Caesar with Pompey's head as a gift.

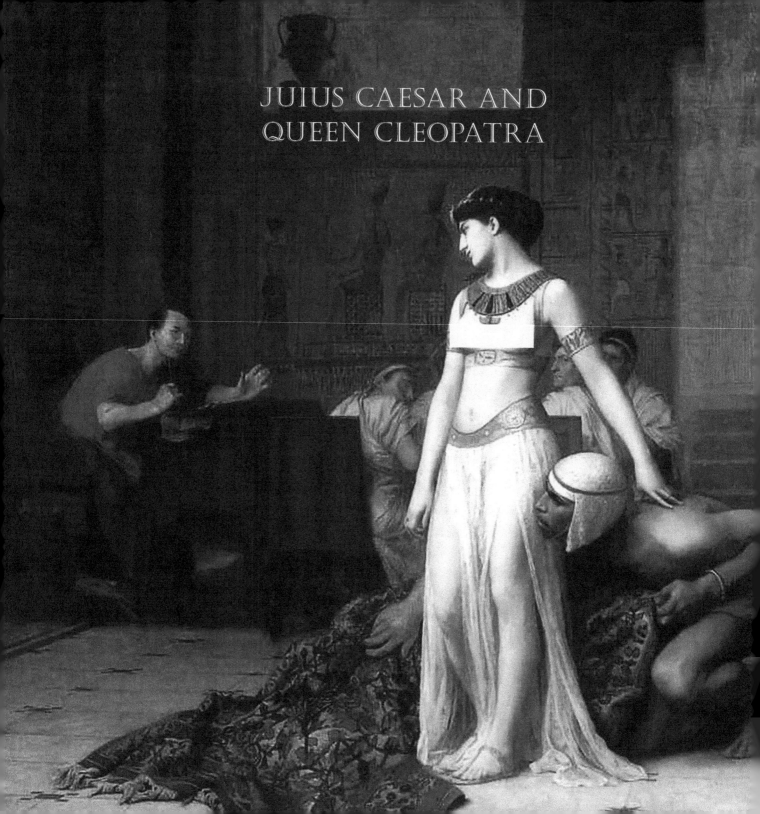

JUIUS CAESAR AND
QUEEN CLEOPATRA

CLEOPATRA

He fell in love with the queen of Egypt, Cleopatra, while he was there. He assisted her in becoming pharaoh and they had a child named Caesarion.

ROMAN DICTATOR

Caesar again returned to Rome in 46 BC, now considered to be the world's most powerful man. He was made dictator for life by the Senate and he ruled like he was the king, making many changes to Rome. He proceeded to name his own supporters to the Senate. He also built new temples and buildings in the City. Julius proceeded to even change the calendar to the famous Julian calendar which included 365 days as well as a leap year.

STATUE OF JULIUS CAESAR

THE MURDER OF CAESAR

MURDER

Some of the Romans thought that he held too much power and they worried his rule would bring the Roman Republic to an end. They decided it was time to kill him and plotted his death. Cassius and Brutus were the leaders of this plot. When he entered the senate on March 15, 44 BC, several men charged him and started attacking him, killing him by stabbing him 23 times.

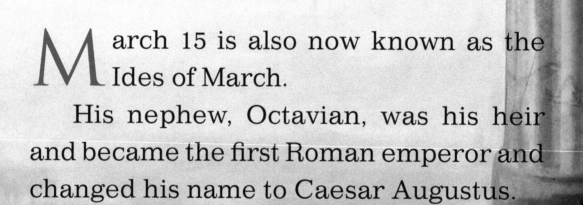

March 15 is also now known as the Ides of March.

His nephew, Octavian, was his heir and became the first Roman emperor and changed his name to Caesar Augustus.

JULIUS CAESAR AND THE IDES
OF MARCH

BRVTVS · CASSIVS · IVLIVS · BRVTVS ·

PORCIA

PORCIA

Vō porcia cathonis vticenſis tochť das lxxix ca ·

AFTER THE ASSASSINATION

The unforeseen results from the assassination was that his death would precipitate the end of the Roman Republic. The lower and middle classes, that Caesar was immensely popular with had become enraged that such a small group of aristocrats had murdered him.

OTHER ROMAN EMPERORS

During Ancient Rome's first 500 years, the government was considered to be a republic and no one person had the ultimate power. For the following 500 years, however, Rome then became an empire which was ruled by its emperor.

MATTHIAS
HOLY ROMAN EMPEROR

HENRY II CROWNED
ROMAN EMPEROR

While several of the republic government offices were still in force, such as the senators, to assist with running the new government, the emperor was considered the supreme leader and often considered to be a god.

THE FIRST ROMAN EMPEROR

Caesar Augustus was the first Roman Emperor. He had several names that included Octavius, but went by Augustus once he was the Emperor. As you learned earlier, he was Julius Caesar's adopted heir.

When Julius Caesar was murdered, Octavius took his place and soon became the first Emperor over the Roman Empire.

OCTAVIUS AUGUSTUS

EMPEROR'S THRONE

STRONG EMPERORS

You might feel that the Roman republic changing to an empire might be a bad idea. This might be true in some cases. In other instances, however, the Emperor was a strong, good leader that brought prosperity and peace to Rome. Some of the better emperors are listed here:

Caesar Augustus – Augustus, the original Emperor, set a great example for the future leaders of Rome. After many years of civil war in Rome, Augustus's rule was known as Pax Romana (Roman peace), a time of peace. He had formed a standing army, rebuilt much of Rome, and created a network of roads in the City.

CAESAR AUGUSTUS

Claudius - Claudius conquered many new areas and started the Britain conquest. In also built several aqueducts, roads and canals.

Marcus Aurelius - Marcus was known as the Philosopher-King. He was not only Emperor, but was also considered to be one of history's leading stoic philosophers. Marcus was the last "Five Good Emperors".

Trajan – According to several historians, Trajan is considered to be the best of Rome's Emperors. He ruled Rome 19 years. It was during that time period that he took over many lands increasing the size and wealth of the empire. He was known to be a determined builder, and constructed several lasting buildings throughout Rome.

Diocletian

Diocletian - Diocletian was perhaps both a bad and a good emperor. As the Empire was getting to be too large to manage from Rome, he split it into two sections; the Western Roman Empire and the Eastern Roman Empire.

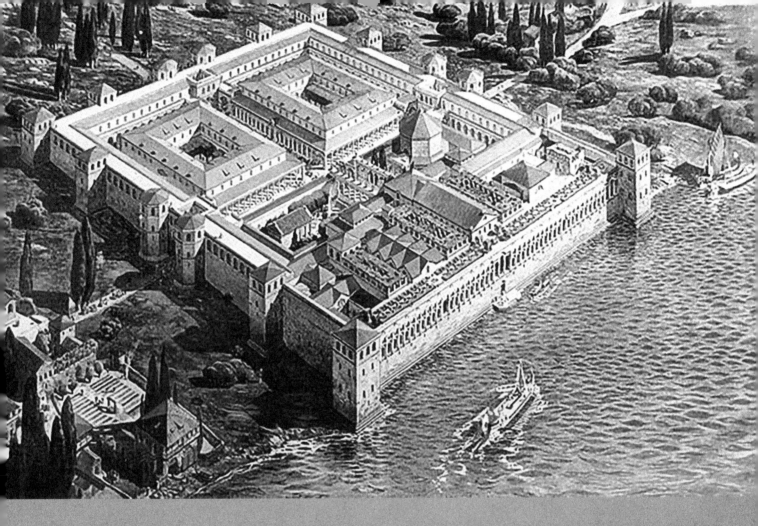

The allowed the massive Empire to be easily ruled and able to defend its surrounding borders. He was however, one of the worst when it came to human rights, persecuting and killing many people, Christians in particular, because of their religious beliefs.

THE CRAZY EMPERORS

Rome had a few crazy emperors too. A few of them include Caligula, Domitian, Commodus and Nero (who was often blamed for the burning of Rome).

Cajus Caligula.

CONSTANTINE

CONSTANTINE THE GREAT

Constantine ruled the Eastern Roman Empire and was the first Emperor that converted to Christianity and began the conversion to Christianity.

In addition, he changed the name of the city of Byzantium to Constantinople, which became the Eastern Roman Empire capital for more than 1000 years.

CONSTANTINOPLE

THE END OF THE ROMAN EMPIRE

The end of the two halves of the Empire occurred at different times. In 476 AD, the Western Empire ended when Romulus Augustus, the last Roman Emperor, was defeated by Odoacer, the German. In 1453 AD, with the fall of Constantinople to the Ottoman Empire, the Eastern Roman Empire came to an end.

ROMULUS AUGUSTULUS
AND ODOACER

Julius Caesar was an accomplished man and he played a major role in events leading up to the end of Roman Republic and the beginning of the Roman Empire.

For additional information about Julius Caesar and the Roman empire, you can go to your local library, research the internet, and ask questions of your teachers, family and friends.

Visit

BABY PROFESSOR
EDUCATION KIDS

www.BabyProfessorBooks.com

to download Free Baby Professor eBooks and view
our catalog of new and exciting Children's Books

CPSIA information can be obtained
at www.ICGtesting.com
Printed in the USA
JSHW051406081222
34213JS00007B/222